The Wisdom of Kindness

The Direction for Living Our Best Life

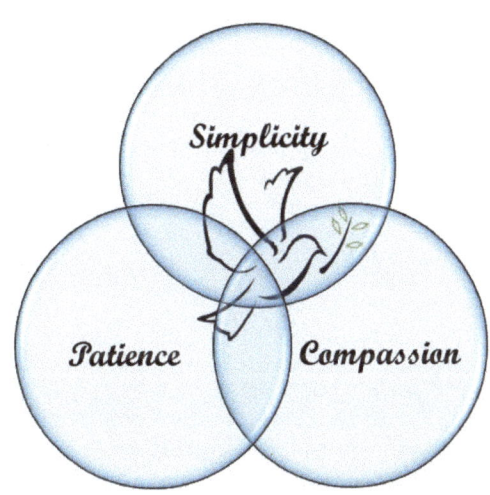

HERB WILLIAMS

RiverHouse Publishing, LLC

The Wisdom of Kindness

Copyright © 2020 by **Herb Williams**

RiverHouse Publishing, LLC
1509 Madison Avenue
Memphis, TN 38104

ISBN: **978-1-7335622-3-2**

All rights reserved. No part of this book may be reproduced, stored in a retrieval system or transmitted in any form or by any means without written permission of the Publisher, excepting brief quotes used in reviews.

All **RiverHouse, LLC** Titles, Imprints and Distributed Lines are available at special quantity discounts for bulk purchases for sales promotions, premiums, fund-raising and educational or institutional use.

www.riverhousepublishingllc.com

DEDICATION

This book is dedicated to all our children and grandchildren, who are on life's journey of learning, maturing and blossoming.

Special appreciation and recognition to all the late bloomers who continue to learn and to teach from their joy.

A New BEGINNING

Your mind is a garden.
Your thoughts are the seeds.
You can grow flowers, or you can grow weeds.
Kindness offers the guide
on how to live.
Wisdom asks that we
accept, receive and give.

(Quote by James Allen)

Table of Contents

Introduction 6

Chapter 1: A New Beginning 60

Chapter 2: The Circle of Kindness 116

    Chapter 3: The Chosen Lens for Thought 118

    Chapter 4: Simply Do Your Best 32

    Chapter 5: Remain Open to Kindness 45

    Chapter 6: The Circle of Kindness Discussion 59

Chapter 7: A Family Tradition of Kindness & Joyful Living 85

Chapter 8: Conclusion for Now 90

References 101

Introduction

> "
> ACCEPT
>
> RECEIVE
>
> GIVE
> "
>
> PROVERB FOR LIVING

Quality, abundance, pleasantness, joyfulness, balance, collaboration, poise and command of this existence are characteristics of a well-lived life. Such things are not goals but describe a lifestyle or a way and a direction for living our best life. Throughout the ages, and across different cultures, it has been rightly shared that, *"life is a journey, not a destination"* and *"knowing thyself is the beginning of all wisdom."* Ultimately, the journey that we undertake is one of re-awakening to truth, *"the exchange of darkness for light and of ignorance for understanding".* Learning and maturity have little to do with age and more to do with the decision to begin living our best life. So, regardless of any situation, circumstance, opinion or documentation, know that each of us are capable and worthy of living a wonderful life. Life lived with the guidance of kindness represents love in action. The abundance of love represents the Creator of life.

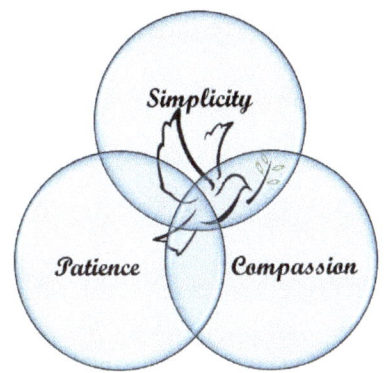

A child in the first grade was asked to make something with the clay that was given to the class as the parents were scheduled to view the work. Being familiar with the activity, the boy began to play with the clay but not in the manner that the teacher had hoped. The teacher began to encourage and to nudge the child to complete the task. She said, okay your mom is going to look in soon, come on, let's make something for her to see. With a clear, spirited, and impassioned tone the little boy said, "I just wanna PLAY WITH it for a minute!!!"

"We are all teachers and learners with more to learn than to teach. And the one that we must teach most frequently is our self." Without the wisdom of kindness, we may not recognize our role in producing environments that promote compliance instead of encouraging excellence. Under wisdom's guidance, we learn how to facilitate, when to step-in and how to encourage ourselves. Only then can we consistently assist another, as it is difficult to give what we have not received. As teachers and learners, our task is to do what is necessary to maintain structure while promoting an environment for excellence. Wisdom, kindness and truth consistently offer each of us the owner's manual for living our best life.

> **Let Your Heart be at Peace.**
>
> *Each separate being in the universe*
> *returns to the common source.*
> *Returning to the source is serenity.*
>
> *If you don't realize the source,*
> *you stumble in confusion and sorrow.*
>
> *When you realize where you come from,*
> *you naturally become tolerant,*
> *kindhearted as a grandmother,*
> *and dignified as a king.*
>
> *Immersed in the wonder and guidance of Love,*
> *You can deal with whatever life brings you.*
>
> (paraphrased from the Tao-te-Ching)

The stories we tell ourselves matter greatly as they serve to orient the direction for our thoughts. However, oftentimes **when we hear wisdom-based stories and teachings, we think the message is for someone else.** Many of us say that we want change, but few consciously initiate the effort to cause change to happen. *"The thing that generates our reality is action."* Therefore, a decision to consistently practice life in the direction of love's light will manifest balanced thinking and quality experiences. We teach ourselves to become serene, calm, and poised of character by releasing the eternal abundance of kindness, joyfulness, patience, decency, and truthfulness from within.

We each have the same wonderful journey of discovery. Every activity of each day is an opportunity to practice bringing our joy or misery to the present. Understand that *"The universe doesn't favor the greedy, the dishonest, or the vicious; although on the surface it may sometimes appear to do so."*

Teachers of kindness from the ages have shared that the universe favors those who utilize the strength of determination, the courage of action, and the persistence of effort to journey in the direction of love's light. The moment that we open ourselves to the thought system of kindness and venture to share its wisdom, is the moment that we begin to live our best life.

"As the physically weak person can make themselves strong by careful and patient training, so the possessor of weak thoughts can make themselves strong by exercising in right thinking."
(James Allen)

Chapter 1: A New Beginning

Consider the following fact, "if we hold our hands over our eyes, we will not see because we are interfering with the laws of seeing. If we deny love, we will not know it because our cooperation is the law of its being." (ACIM)

Wisdom is the understanding and acceptance of reality as it presents itself, not as we'd like it to be. Let's acknowledge the fact that we did not make the day, the sun will rise again without our help and within our hearts recognize that the Creator of life has not abandoned Its creation. So, relax and know that in reality, the earth is a place of abundance and we are loved far beyond the boundaries of opinion and belief. Regardless of the thoughts which are currently occupying the mind, in truth we are forever surrounded by kindness, patience, joy and love. With a bit of effort and practice, we can learn to live a consistently joyous life as joy is our home-state of mind.

It appears that life's journey has been structured so that each of us must recognize for ourselves that we are among the vessels for grace and mercy to be shared in the universe. With the decision of maturity, we slowly open our thoughts to the wisdom of kindness. Kindness is more than the qualities of being friendly, generous, and considerate. It has depth of meaning and is like a directional compass that is woven into the fabric of a larger universal thought-system of inclusiveness. Once accepted and received, the thought-system of kindness instantly helps to orient the mind's thinking in the direction of love's ever-present light.

It has been shared that there are only two emotions; love and fear. One was given to us and the other we made. **"Each is a way of seeing, and different worlds arise from their different visions."** With the practice of each activity, conversation and life experience, we train the mind to accept direction for thought from the guidance of fearfulness or lovingkindness. Here, we offer yet another voice in favor of the simplicity and wisdom of *directional thinking*. Utilized properly, the thought-system of kindness can illuminate our journey with greater clarity. It's a though-system which offers insight and understanding of our true identity, encourages inclusiveness and promotes purpose.

"There is but one shift in perception that is necessary, for we made but one mistake. It seems like many, but it is all the same. What is not love is always fear and nothing else." **(ACIM)**

Just as each baby will walk when it is ready, each of us will mature and blossom into the joy of living our best life when we are ready. Both the baby walking and our living joyfully require commitment, effort and daily practice. Though the eyes only witness the outward effects, the seeds of thought first grow within.

Unfortunately, we seem to be far to tolerant of dark thoughts and an untrained mind results in immature thinking. All wisdom-based learning leads towards the decision to look within ourselves for lovingkindness, instead of searching outwardly toward the world. The maturation process is an intimate journey where each one eventually decides to grow-up within the Self.

We share wisdom-based stories in hopes of inspiring additional thoughts, conversations and truth-based discussions. Understand that wisdom does not ask for our belief, it only asks that we try its direction for joyous living. The following short story titled, "A Man Lost His Keys" is worthy of our consideration.

"A MAN LOST HIS KEYS"

One night, a man was in his house with his keys in hand. The lights went out and he dropped the keys. He got down on his hands and knees and began looking for them. The man looked up and noticed that the streetlights outside were on. Rather than grope around in the dark, he decided to go outside to look for his keys under the lights.

A neighbor saw the man outside looking around. He walked over and asked, what he was doing. The man explained that he had lost his keys and was looking for them. The neighbor said okay, I'll help you find them. Now both were searching for the keys under the streetlights. After a short time of searching, the neighbor asked, approximately where did you lose your keys. The man said, I lost them inside the house. The neighbor laughed and asked, okay, why are you looking for them out here? The man explained that it was dark, lonely and uncertain inside. I saw the streetlights and decided to search outside were things seem to be clearer. (paraphrased story by Wayne Dyer)

Before judging the man to harshly, one moral of the story is that when confronted with problems, most if not all of us tend to look outside of ourselves. By looking outside, we teach ourselves to blame others or outside circumstances for problems or challenges that are best resolved by looking within. Understand that **"all challenges seen and unseen lie within our thinking."** We, like the man with the lost keys, are reluctant or afraid to look within as we perceive it as being dark, lonely and uncertain.

Our reluctance to consistently look within for guidance and joyfulness, opens the door of imbalance, unfulfilling pursuit and the teachings of the getting concept. Lacking proper balance, the upside-down world of constantly wanting more stuff and things is fuel for the mental virus of greed.

This contagious mental illness helps to promote the fear-based economy of scarcity. The results are perceptions of misery, unhappiness, helplessness and a disregard for the wellbeing of life.

For consistency of joy, we must train our mind to recognize thoughts, words, and actions which are sourced from the guidance of love and release those without love's light. *"A main purpose for our learning is to enable us to bring the peace with us and to heal distress and turmoil."* Train the mind and it will serve us wonderfully. Fail to train it, then thoughts of lack, want, misery and despair enter the uncared-for space.

Each day is a new day, a new beginning. Another opportunity to grow, to mature and to renew the journey of living our best life.

==

Wisdom-based stories are more than intellectual thoughts or entertaining expressions. *They are like signposts that point the way to a better way.* **Possibly, the greatest adventure within each life's journey is the maturing, the opening up, the growing and the blossoming process itself.** So, for whom does the bell of wisdom and kindness toll? Know that it tolls for thee.

Words, conversations, books, songs and art are wonderful tools which help to orient and direct our thinking. What we allow ourselves to think matters greatly and *"as a person*

thinketh in their heart" so goes their perception of reality. Here, we join two grandparents who have decided to introduce their grandchildren to the long tradition of wisdom-based education, discussions and conversations. To jump-start the discussions, they decided to share a small unfinished book titled *"The Circle of Kindness"* with the grandkids. The small book contained several simple yet thought provoking stories as it was designed to promote more dialog around the subject of living our best life.

The Circle of Kindness
The Prophet, the Preacher and the People

Chapter 2: The Circle of Kindness

"Light does not attack darkness, but it does shine it away." (ACIM)

Many had recognized the almost universal need for more open-minded, plain-spoken, practical, family and community-based discussions where everyday people gather to share insight and exchange ideas on fundamental life-enhancing items. There seemed to be a collective and persistent yearning for exploration and consideration on how to share and to utilize the lore, the learnings and the wisdom from the ages in experiencing the consistency of joy during life's daily journey.

The Circle of Kindness was co-created as a communal learning venue where the participants practice listening to and learning from the best of one another with kindness as the foundation for discernment. While similar in concept to other social gatherings, the C of K discussions are informal, relaxed, collaborative learning environments that helped to orient the participants thinking away from darkness and towards the light.

As such, their positive energy promotes even greater clarity regarding the direction for living one's best life.

True to the circle's inclusive appeal, there's no membership to join, no dues to pay and the primary cost is the courage to bring one's joy while releasing the shackles of fear-based thoughts. The Circle of Kindness discussions continue to grow in popularity as a go-to resource for positive energy and favorable solutions in helping to uplift the individual's perspective and sense of belonging.

Marty became aware of the growing communication platform, attended a few sessions and decided to begin hosting the discussions. He recognized that when we listen to the best of one another and respond with appropriate follow-up actions, the light of humanity and life seem to shine more brightly.

The wisdom of kindness offers guidance and vision for living our best life. Every activity, situation and interaction that comes to our awareness offer lessons of wisdom for accepting, receiving and sharing. With the vision of kindness, we learn to open ourselves to the joy within each situation. Even if we choose not to welcome them, the eternal presence of truth, peacefulness, and joy quietly await our acceptance.

Chapter 3: The Chosen Lens for Thought

While waiting at a transit stop, a stranger is innocently standing near a young lady who is speaking to someone on the phone.

Young lady: You know, I'm just having such a difficult time with seemingly simple things. Looks like each day brings a new set of troubles with it. When does the fun part of life start again? *(She listens as the other person responds to her query.)*

Young Lady: That's a good point. I guess I'm just tired and feeling a bit sorry for myself. But people simply don't appreciate quality anymore. I go out of my way to help some of them and a few don't even bother to say thank you. Maybe they think you owe them something. *(She listens as the other person responds to her comments.)*

Young Lady: Right, I understand. I'm not sure what to do either. But is it asking too much to have decent conversations with adults that care enough to seek understanding? *(She listens a bit more and responds.)*

Young Lady: Okay, sure. Yes, I'll stay open for possibility and change. Thank you for listening and I'll see you soon. Take care.

(The call ends. She attempts to place the phone in her handbag, but it falls to the floor and lands near another waiting passenger's foot. The stranger picks up the phone, smiles and hands it to the young lady.)

Young Lady: Thank you. It's been one of those days. Nope, it's been one of those few weeks. You know what I mean?

Stranger: I understand. Throughout life we sometimes allow the liquid drama of the world to enter our peaceful place. When our mental vessel or mind is distracted with drama, it makes for eventful and sometimes unpleasant life experiences.

Young Lady: That's an interesting way of looking at things. So, what should we do when the "liquid drama" of the world enters our mental vessel? Because I'm ready for my ship to come in.

Stranger: Ah, yes. Are you familiar with the riddle of the two ships who left the harbor at the same time?

Young Lady: Ah, maybe. Please refresh my memory.

Stranger: **Two ships leave the harbor at the same time; one has its course charted and sails in the direction of the desire destination. The second ship didn't map a course and set sails in a seemingly random direction. Which ship will arrive at its destination?**

Young Lady: Well, it appears that both ships will reach their destination. The one that knows where it wants to go is very likely to accomplish its goal. And the one that's headed nowhere in particular will arrive there also. If you're headed nowhere, you can get there quickly, or you can drift about for a very long time. Still, both reach the planned and undocumented goals.

Stranger: Well done and well said. The **power of decision** is also demonstrated by the captains of both ships. One decides to chart her course and the other decides to see what happens. It is possible for both to enjoy their chosen experience. Regardless of our chosen path for adventure, *we can decide to bring our joy or our misery to each life activity.* With this decision, we consciously or unconsciously **establish the direction for our daily living.**

Young Lady: I'm not sure that I've "decided" the direction for daily living before. Is this something that you've done?

Stranger: It certainly took many, many years before slowing down enough to recognize and accept the **concept of directional thinking**. Each day brings more awareness to the living-truth of life that continues to uplift and enlighten with its presence in every moment.

Young Lady: Again, that's an interesting way of wording things and I'm not sure that I fully understand what you mean by "the living-truth of life". Many say that there is no absolute truth and that it's relative to a particular frame of reference. Too hear folks talk today, the truth has become like beauty "it's in the eye of the beholder".

Stranger: You are correct that two people can read the same passage or see the same incident and present two very different perspectives. We understand that this is largely **due to the lens or manner in which we allow ourselves to view a situation.** The story of *The Blind Men and the Elephant* demonstrates this truth. However, there's no denying the truth of life, which is presented in countless forms, shapes and sizes.

Young Lady: Okay, you're referring to the presence of life as "the living-truth of life". I understand. You're right. The basic presence or "the living-truth of life" is all around us and it's undeniable. But still, growing up in my neighborhood, when two people gave different stories about the same event, we would say that one of them was just lying.

Stranger: It is possible that during discussion, one or more of the participants may have elected to practice naughtiness or deceit. However, each of us have thought one thing and later learned that we were mistaken regarding our limited perception of the issue. If we pay attention, often **the lessons that are offered** as a result of the situation are much more important than a declaration of individual right or wrong. A more beneficial approach might be related **to how we can become better as a result of the situation. As every activity, conversation or situation is a learning opportunity.**

Young Lady: Okay, what's the learning opportunity when you're surrounded by people who are ungrateful and lack appreciation for the things you've already done and continue to do for them? They don't care about the financial and health sacrifices that have been and continue to be made on their behalf. Help me with the optimism in these situations.

Stranger: Our concerns contain opportunities to grow and to **consciously re-establish commitment to living our best life.** We each have an abundance of gifts that must be shared freely without the attachment of external gratitude in order to be most beneficial.

Young Lady: I'm not following you. What gifts are you talking about? And when it comes to gratitude, is it asking too much for someone to say thank you. Or, I appreciate your help?

Stanger: As we allow ourselves to grow and to mature, our appreciation for pleasantness, peace of mind and thriving within life increase in value. When we practice living from the abundance of kindness, patience and the power of forgiveness, *we free our mind from the belief that acceptance, appreciation or approval from outside forces are desired or required.* The gifts of kindness and forgiveness unlock the shackles of despair while reminding us to remember the importance of home.

Young Lady: Are you a minister, a preacher or something like that?

Stranger: No Ma'am. I am just like you. Just a person trying to consistently find the way home regardless of the situation.

Young Lady: I'm sorry, find your way home. Are you lost?

Stranger: We all lose our way from time to time. So, each day is another opportunity to **learn the importance of practicing excellence with life**.

Young Lady: I didn't expect that response. Usually, when someone admits to being lost, they show signs of worry, anxiety and fear.

Stranger: If asked, most adults will confirm their familiarity with such dark and fear-based thoughts. When we recognize that we are away from home, the choice is to remain in darkness or return to our center. The path becomes clearer as we open ourselves **to the idea of living our best life**. The liberation and freedom of life's eternal light awaits all who care enough to seek.

Young Lady: Well alright. That sounds like a worthy journey. Is there any electric-juice, or cloudy-head-yazoo involved?

Stranger: Please pardon me. I don't understand.

Young Lady: Don't worry about it. It's old neighborhood slang. So, it appears that you have a handle on things. You know a lot of people talk about living their best life but other than a sound bite or two, few follow up with practical how-to information. Beyond the generic rhetoric, do you offer something of substance like a formula for living? How do we live our best life?

Stranger: Let's start with home. The decision regarding the state of one's home is most important. Remember the saying, "compassion starts at home and then spreads abroad." There's a short story that illustrates how **our home-state of mind travels with us**. It's well-known and you may be familiar with it.

Young Lady: I believe the saying is "charity starts at home". But that's okay, compassion can be considered inclusive of charity. Let's hear the story.

Stranger: *Long, long ago, an old man was sitting under a tree near the entrance to a town. Two young children were playing in the tree and overheard the advice that was shared with two families as they approached the town.*

The first family asked, "Hello Sir, what kind of people live in this town? We've decided to relocate and start a new life?"

The old man replied, "What kind of people lived in your last town?"

The father replied, "They were unfriendly, dishonest and just plain mean-spirited folks. That's why we decided to move."

The old man replied, "Well, you'll find some of those same kind of folks in this town."

The family said thank you and traveled into the town.

A short time later, another family stopped in front of the tree and asked, "Hello Sir, what kind of people live in this town?"

The old man replied, "What kind of people lived in your last town?"

The father replied, "The people were friendly and kind. We had grown close just like an extended family. We're relocating as part of a business agreement."

The old man replied, "Well, you'll find some of those same kind of folks in this town."

The family said thank you and traveled into the town.

The children climbed out of the tree and ask the old man, "Why did you tell those people two different things?"

The old man replied, "I was truthful to both families. Understand that we attract and see the things that reflect our accepted mode of thinking. Our home state of mind travels with us wherever we go. We each must learn to change our lens for thought towards the light of kindness. As our thinking is a way of seeing and the eyes will retrieve what the mind dwells upon."

Young Lady: Yes, I've heard the story before. Although it was a little bit different and the concluding message was not exactly the same.

Stranger: What seems to be many choices may prove to be a choice between just two. To live our best life, we need only **decide to consistently think** and therefore live from a thought system of kindness which is opposite the temptation of fear.

Young Lady: So, that's it? That's your formula for living our best life? Think from the position of kindness?

Stranger: In this case, **kindness is considered synonymous with love, joy and compassion.** The decision to redirect our thinking and to practice living from the vantage of kindness is significant as *all life's experiences are considered an inside job*. With respect to free will of decision, might there be a formula any simpler than **a two directional compass for thinking and living**? The chosen guide and direction for thought influences every aspect of our perceptions.

Young Lady: A two directional compass for thinking and living. I hear what you're saying, but I'm not sure that I completely follow your idea. And for a person with a way with words, surely you can offer a bit more detail than that.

Stranger: The principled thoughts and concepts being shared are not mine. They represent the many timeless gifts from the ages and are as important to our growth as the current is to the river. **Understand that wisdom-based ideas and concepts are not to be believed. We are asked to simply try or test their guidance for truth.**

(The northbound train quickly comes into view and arrives on schedule.)

Young Lady: Sure. But can you share a few more details for living our best life?

Stranger: A proper response requires more of an ongoing dialog. However, experiencing a wonderful life likely begins with one's decision to seek more wisdom-based education. Proper education brings awareness to the truth of the Self beyond the small identities of I. Next, establish positive habits to nurturing your essential infrastructure items such as *drinking clean water, healthy eating, reasonable sleeping, regular exercise, daily meditation, and the practice of directional thinking*. With understanding of our home-state of being, these things will allow each person to blossom as a wonderful representation of life.

Young Lady: Well alright. You said a mouthful and it made reasonable sense. Thank you for an interesting conversation.

Stanger: Thank you kindly for a joyful experience. Take care.

(Both board the train and with limited seating they find seats that are a few rows apart. The train pulls off towards the midtown station.)

After a few additional stops, the train car was full as a few people remained standing. There was a small commotion between two passengers regarding the availability of a seat. In a final attempt to defuse the situation, another passenger stood-up and offered the irate man his seat. The man refused the offer and insisted that the objects in the seat in question should be removed.

The train pulled into the midtown station and many of the passengers existed the train.

(The Young Lady walks over to the Stranger after existing the train.)

Young Lady: Well hello stranger. *(They both share a laugh.)*

Stranger: It's a wonderful day to be alive, well and free.

Young Lady: I agree. The commute would have been better without the "liquid drama" of bickering. Who do you think was right? The man who wanted the items removed from the seat or the women who placed all her stuff there first?

Stranger: Right or wrong in any situation might be debatable however, the kindness of the gentleman who offered his seat is an example of behavior worthy of our emulation.

Young Lady: Yea, I agree that he made a kind gesture. But regarding the two arguing, who was right?

Stranger: Life consistently presents opportunities for learning. We could learn to be more grateful as **people provide examples of things to do, things not to do, and opportunity to share our treasures.**

Young Lady: Okay, I think I like that. Now, did you agree with the lady and her stuff or the man insisting that she move it?

Stranger: When we learn to consistently practice directional-thinking, awareness of life lessons beyond right or wrong begin to add positive depth, appreciation and joy to most experiences. Such are the benefits of our home-state of being.

Young Lady: Okay, I have a scheduled appointment as you may, but you've repeatedly mentioned the concept of home, home-state of mind, and home-state of being. Please help me understand your position a bit more clearly.

Stranger: Our true home-state of being is with us at birth, journeys with us throughout life and likely transcends the realm of our limited perception. The foundation of our home-state is that of pleasant joyfulness. All other behavior may be perceived as playful folly, misguided energy or mistaken learning.

Young Lady: Are you a psychologist or a psychiatrist?

Stranger: Not at all. I'm just like any other. One who's trying to consistently find the way home regardless of the situation. It is common knowledge that we all are capable of error. **With understanding of directional thinking, when we recognize the mental state of anger, worry or despair, we can more quickly and easily re-direct our thinking towards the light of kindness. It helps to expose the choice of madness as an option of nothingness.**

Young Lady: It sounds like your home-state of being is the same as mindset. Like the person who chooses to wear the rose-colored glasses.

Stranger: That's one way to look at it. Those who have decided to mature will likely choose to wear the rose-colored lens of compassion while the misguided or undecided drift about with dark shades of fear. Both have selected a companion and guide for thought, meaning and therefore living.

Young Lady: Okay, I mostly understand your vibe. Might you have another example of what you're saying?

Stranger: Know that our thoughts are powerful as they direct the instrument of the eyes to retrieve images which reflect our chosen companion for thinking. Again, like truth, such wisdom-based teachings have been with us for thousands of years. They ask not for belief but honest exploration and sincere evaluation.

Young Lady: Okay, I don't believe any of it and will evaluate the thoughts. I'm also running short of time before my appointment. So, do you have an example of what you're saying?

Stranger: One teacher shared the following example in referencing "The Hand."

The hand in its natural state, absent any pain or when not being used to express excitement or anger, is demonstrating pleasantness. Meaning, when the hand is simply being a hand just as it was created, it is relaxed, calm, ready and available to follow the direction of the mind.

Recognize that those situations when the hand is instructed to express excitement or anger are not sustainable positions. Realize that both imposters, the party happy hands and the fighting mad hands must eventually release the temporary emotion at some point.

With that said, the hand's natural and home-state of calmness, pleasantness and peacefulness also applies to the instrument of the mind.

Young Lady: Okay, it's been really nice talking with you. I glean the following from your message. Our accepted guide for thinking (whether kind or unkind) impacts

the perception of all life experiences and the eyes see what the trained mind has been led to think. Thank you for sharing and I hope to see around.
(She waves goodbye as she begins walking away.)

Stranger: Thank you kindly.   *(The Stranger waves and journeys in a different direction.)*

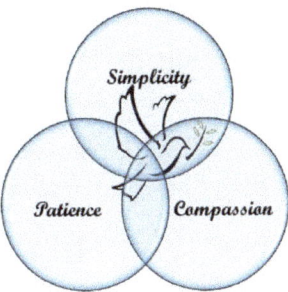

"Resolve to understand and know who we really are. Once knowledge is gained regarding our true Self, we will better understand all others and be more tolerant of misguided energies and behaviors."

Chapter 4: Simply Do Your Best

A young boy bouncing a ball loses control of it. The ball rolls across the street landing near a passing stranger. The passerby picks it up, navigates the oncoming traffic and returns the ball.

Boy: Thank you, I was afraid that one of the cars was going to hit my ball.

Passerby: You are most welcome my friend.

Boy: Why do you call me friend? You don't even know my name.

Passerby: Oh, that's an easy one. Have you heard the saying, *"The lamps are different, but the light is the same"*?

Boy: No Sir. I'm not sure that I even know what it means.

Passerby: Oh, sure you do. Is there more than one lamp or light fixture in your family's house?

Boy: Uhmm, I think so. Yes, yes. There's more than one lamp in our house.

Passerby: Okay, even though the lamps may be of different shapes, sizes, and colors, the light is the same as it comes from the same source.

Boy: And that's why you called me friend?

Passerby: Yes. The saying reminds us that **the spirit of life within every person is from the same source.** So, when I recognized that you needed a little help, I saw you as a friend who could use a helping hand.

Boy: Okay. Thank you again.

Passerby: You're welcome again.

Boy: Do you play basketball? It's my favorite sport.
Passerby: It was once most enjoyable. Basketball and other sports can be a wonderful vehicle for learning important lessons.

Boy: You mean lessons like how to dribble and shoot better?

Passerby: The excitement for the game is clearly felt through your words. And there's nothing wrong with that. We may agree that basketball is just one part of many activities that make up our life. Activities like reading, learning, communicating, giving and helping others are worthy of our attention. You see?

Boy: Yeah, I understand. There's more to life than basketball.

Passerby: Hold on a moment. Let's recognize our shared truth. We also agreed that basketball can be a wonderful vehicle for learning and teaching some important life lessons. We simply must **remember to keep the main thing as the main thing.**

Boy: What do you mean the main thing?

Passerby: The main thing is to teach ourselves how to live a joyful, kind and purposeful life that contributes to the greater good for all. What if, the lessons or technics used to improve basketball skills could be used to improve your life experiences. Would you be interested in learning a few of them?

Boy: Anything that can help improve my hooping skills. Right now, I don't get to play much because the other kids are much better than me.

Passerby: Not a problem. You're doing the right thing by practicing. Whenever we want to improve at something, the actions of consistent practice, commitment of will and our best effort bring positive results. Practice makes you what?

Boy: Practice makes you perfect!

Passerby: Well, how about better. **Practice makes us better.** And when we consistently practice a thing by simply doing our best, we become better at the focused thing. To bring your best to each practice is also a form of practicing excellence. And a person who is practicing excellence at something may become outstanding or extremely good. What do you think?

Boy: I think that I'm going to be an excellent basketball player.

Passerby: If that's your goal, then an excellent basketball player you shall be. Now, we were discussing technics for improving life skills that can also contribute to your basketball talents.

Boy: Right.

Passerby: Okay, an important item in helping to improve our life and any other skill is **the decision to thrive and not just survive.** A decision to thrive is a decision to grow and to mature regardless of the circumstances or the situation. Understand that all activities are presented for us to become better and not bitter. So, **never worry or concern yourself with the talents of another or the things you don't have. Most of the time, we already have far more than what is needed to thrive.**

Boy: Thrive? What do you mean, thrive?

Passerby: That's a wonderful question. To survive is to just get by, to thrive is to grow in a healthy manner, to prosper, to flourish, to blossom and to win with life while helping others.

Boy: Yeah. I want to win.

Passerby: Remember, to win with life is to simply **practice bringing our joy and best effort to every experience.** Don't concern yourself with being good or not so good. Simply allow yourself to enjoy the experience of the activity while utilizing quality form and methods. Because when we focus our energies and consistently practice a thing, the joy of practice makes us what?

Boy: Makes us perfect. No. I mean better.

Passerby: Exactly. If we practice sound technics in basketball or life, we become better and journey towards excellence. **It all starts with our decision, then our commitment to joyful practice.**

Boy: Is that all to it?

Passerby: That's mostly it. And I'll share this important word with you. The word is **integrity**. To practice and to live a life of **integrity means to consistently do what you say you're going to do.** For example, if you say you're going to practice your basketball skills for 90 minutes and then read for 90 minutes 5 days a week, then you should do just that.

Boy: I like basketball, but I don't like reading. What does reading have to do with becoming a good basketball player?

Passerby: Well remember, **the main thing is to teach ourselves how to live joyfully while contributing to the greater good of life.** In fact, all activities are part of life's educational process. So, basketball when combined with reading is a wonderful learning vehicle capable of teaching very important life lessons. The excellence gained in reading is transferable or can cross-over into other areas like basketball.

Boy: Yeah. And I want to learn more about the cross-over.

Passerby: Okay, if you improve your basketball and reading skills you can help the team perform better and win in different ways.

Boy: Everybody likes to play on the winning teams.

Passerby: True. Teams are made up of individuals and the individuals must learn, practice and study to be most effective. Remember, it's **important for us to train our mind to think kindly and become a person of our word.** A basketball team with people of integrity is a winning team because they consistently do their best.

Boy: Sure, I'll do my best.

Passerby: Please don't overlook the important reading part. It will help you become a very valuable team member.

Boy: But I just don't like it. It's hard and no fun.

Passerby: When we shoot the ball towards the basket, we miss the shot as much as we make it. But we understand that if we keep trying and keep practicing, we'll experience greater improvements in our game. Practice makes us what?

Boy: Practice makes us better.

Passerby: We bounce the ball over and over in different ways in order to become more comfortable and familiar with it. Repetition of a desired task, activity or skill is most important to the learning process. So, whether we're learning to read, to communicate properly or aspiring to upgrade any other life skill, **it's the consistent repetition of practice that helps us to grow and to improve**. It's easy, simply remember integrity and always do your best. If you practice these things, excellence is in your future.

Boy: I guess you're right. I'll try my best.

Passerby: To help with our learning, life offers each of us a job. It's an important and most useful job.

Boy: What kind of job? Am I too young?

Passerby: You're never too young or too old for this job. In a way, everybody should consider it as part of their life's job description.

Boy: What is it? What's the job?

Passerby: Okay, the job and the title are the same, but the tasks can be anything. Before I share the job with you, I'd like to tell you a short story.

Boy: Can you tell me about the job first? You said that everybody should have this job. What's the job?

Passerby: Okay, this job is a gift. And like any good gift, if we learn to properly utilize it and share it with other people, even greater benefits are received. **The title of the job is called "doing my best".**

Boy: Huh?

Passerby: That's right. "Doing my best" is the only job that we should fully embrace. Although the tasks of life may change, our inwardly accepted job title remains the same. For example, whether you're playing basketball or reading, if someone asks, what are you doing? You can honestly say, I'm "doing my best".

Boy: I like it. My job is to do my best.

Passerby: That's right. And no one can ask that you do more than your best. **When we bring our best effort to each task, we begin the process of practicing excellence.** It's important to practice excellence as we'll grow stronger just in time to help another in need. When we help another, we automatically help ourselves.

Boy: Practice and always do my best.

Passerby: Now you understand how the same technics used to excel in basketball can be used to improve reading and other life skills. Simply do your best and be true to yourself which is to practice life with integrity.

Boy: Okay, be true to my word.

Passerby: Here's another way to **remember integrity**. Always try to **do the right thing**, especially when you're by yourself.

Boy: When I'm by myself? Why?

Passerby: It's for the best possible reason of all and that's because you are always watching. And you are a very important person to yourself. You are most important to "this one" (meaning yourself). And each of us are most important to the universe.

Boy: Yea, I guess so. My grandma tells us to, **"do the right thing and the right thing will follow."**

Passerby: Your grandma is correct. So, when you practice integrity, remember to bring your joy and simply do your best, then you are practicing excellence. This works for basketball and for any of life's activities.

Boy: Alright. I'll practice reading. But some time I forget the things that I just read. Should I still read?

Passerby: There are many, many things that we aren't able to instantly remember but we still live and benefit from them. For example, we don't remember being born but we're pretty confident that it happened. *(They both share a small laugh.)*

Passerby: When we practice living life activities with integrity and doing our best, really good things follow. There's a short story that shows how the small things in life accumulate, grow and add up to important things.

Boy: Okay, I'm ready for the story.

Passerby: The story is called "The Beachfront of Your Life".

The Beachfront of Your Life

It is reasonable to agree that beachfront property (for example Miami beach) is some of the most expensive real estate in the world.

It is also reasonable to agree that we can go visit the beach, fill our pockets with sand and bring some of the beach home with us. (Do you agree?)

How is it true that we can bring some of the most expensive property in the world home with us, without general concern?

It's because individually, the grains of sand are viewed as ordinary, in abundance, and therefore not as important. Yet they add-up to create some of the most expensive real estate in the world.

What does this mean to you and me?

Well, each decision we make adds up to create the beachfront of our life. Our decisions to be kind, to go to school, to study, to eat a healthy diet, to exercise, to forgive or to simply brush our teeth and many other seemingly ordinary or isolated decisions combine to create the beachfront of our life's experiences.

Individually and isolated, the decisions don't appear to have much value or impact. However, they combine to create the quality and perceived beachfront of our lives.

Herb-Will

Passerby: Did the story make sense?

Boy: Yeah. When we do the right thing, they add up to bigger things.

Passerby: That's right. It's an important lesson because only you are responsible for maintaining your joy in life. So, be sure to balance your basketball practice with reading practice. You'll soon learn that reading and learning is as enjoyable as basketball.

Boy: Okay, I'm going to practice basketball and reading. Then, my winning team will make lots of money.

Passerby: Best wishes to you my friend. Keep learning and be open to receive our 3 great human treasures. They are most helpful during life's journey also.

Boy: Treasure. What treasure?

Passerby: All humans have access to 3 great treasures that are capable of leading each person toward a joy filled life. **Our wonderful human treasures are simplicity, patience, and compassion.**

Boy: I thought you meant real treasures like money or gold.

Passerby: Oh, my friend, with acceptance and sharing of these treasures, we become better prepared to enjoy the currency and riches of the day. These treasures bring an internal wealth that positively influences all activities.

Boy: But I thought that everybody wanted more money.

Passerby: You're right in thinking that many spend a lot of time pursuing worldly riches and completely overlook the wisdom in simplicity, the teachings of patience and the joyful freedom found within compassion.

Boy: I'm not sure that I understand.

Passerby: That's okay. If you can remember that most things can be simplified (made easier to do), practice patience (practice keeping your cool and know that things will get better) and teach yourself about the power of compassion (which is related to kindness). If you do these things, then the proper amount of financial rewards will find their way to you.

Boy: Is that right? Just practice the 3 treasures and I'll become rich?

Passerby: These treasures add to our tools and resources for living our best life. Simply practice bringing our joy while "doing our best" in every activity. By thinking and behaving in this direction the rewards of life will come to you.

Boy: Yes, Sir. Practice life and basketball with integrity.

Passerby: Remember, the goal of life is not to best an opponent at basketball or at life. **The goal is to practice being the best that you can be while living a joyful life with integrity and kindness as your guide.**

(The passerby begins to walk away.)

Passerby: Now, don't be surprised if the riches flow from other areas that you're practicing excellence like your reading.

Boy: Okay. Thank you.

Passerby: Thank you my friend. Relax, enjoy the process and practice improving life's activities. What you do does matter and if you simply do your best, you'll show up just in time to really help another in a significant way.

Chapter 5: Remain Open to Kindness

Marty is busy preparing for the community discussion by arranging the dozen or so seats in the usual circle. He's a confident and fair-minded young man in his early forties. Just six months earlier he was an associate at a small non-profit organization in the mid-town area. He wants to help others find the way to a consistently joyful life while answering the question, "is it possible?" for himself.

Marty began hosting a weekly open community forum with kindness as its primary foundation. A welcome banner which reads; "Community Circle of Kindness, Everyone is Welcome!" hangs as the entrance.

A sudden burst of wind blows a few loose papers out towards the street. An unknown man picks up the documents and returns them to Marty.

Unknown man: Hello Sir, it appears that these documents may belong to you.

Marty: Yes, thank you. You never know what the wind's going to do. I must be more careful. How are you today?

Unknown man: I'm well. Thank you kindly for asking. Your welcome banner is inviting. It would be an honor to assist you with something.

(Marty thought about it a moment and with a friendly smile responded.)

Marty: I need help getting rid of this persistent pain in my back and this nagging headache that shows up from time to time. While you're at it, can you help me shed a few of these extra pounds? Oh yea, one more thing. Do you know how one can get a handle on the mental wondering of the mind? Sometimes the craziest thoughts seem to come from nowhere.

Unknown man: Well, I must say that you have shared some potentially transformative requests. My response is yes. It is possible.

Marty: I agree. Our possibilities and potentials are unlimited. The problem is that we've mostly forgotten to live from this perspective. Have a seat. This communal palace is always open and no one's a stranger.

Unknown man: To properly respond to your question, it may take a minute or so.

Marty: Honestly brother, I was only kidding with that list of troubles.

Unknown man: Still, it would be nice to exchange some good ideas on the topics.

Marty: Sure. And if you have a few, I'll be happy to listen. What's your name?

Unknown man: Most folks call me John-jon.

Marty: Cool, thanks for stopping by and for sharing your insight John-jon. The people call me a few different names, but I prefer Marty.

John-jon: Pleased to meet you Marty. *(They shake hands.)* The concerns that you mentioned were mostly of a physical nature and then you wisely added the symptom of misguided thoughts. It is possible that each of the concerns are related and can be better addressed with understanding of one principle.

Marty: Once again my friend, I was only kidding around with you. I don't expect you to help me with these things. However, I am interested in this principle. So, please proceed.

THE LAW OF LAWS, CAUSE AND EFFECT

John-jon: Just because one is kidding doesn't mean that the request or statement is undesired or invalid. It is possible that our physical and mental concerns may be explained and possibly resolved with understanding of this one principle. Some call it a tool, a universal law or the law of laws. It's the law of **cause and effect.**

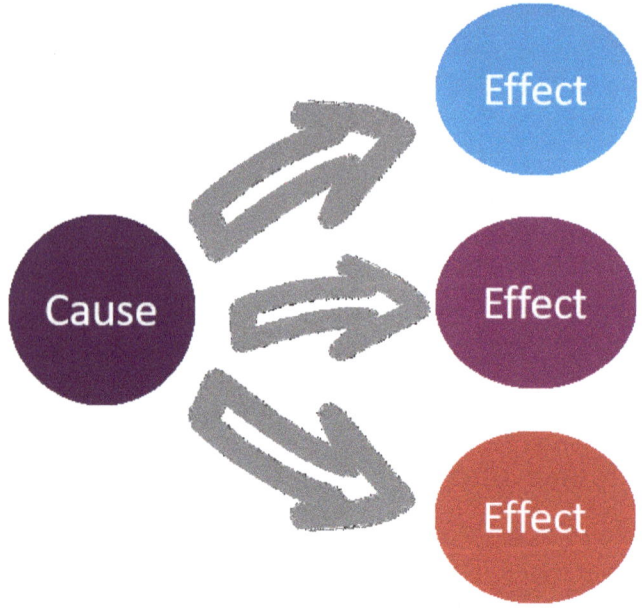

Marty: Okay, I am familiar with this concept or law. It's very similar to the principle of reaping and sowing. Right? "You reap what you sow." I agree that it's a powerful and beneficial lesson for us to learn. If you sow or plant watermelon seeds, under the proper conditions, it's reasonable to expect watermelons to grow. Therefore, we're all encouraged to do our part in sowing more seeds of goodwill and kindness towards one another.

John-jon: Well said. If we consistently teach and train our mind to think in the direction of kindness and inclusiveness the rewards of peace of mind, pleasantness and joy are the resulting fruit. Each cause has effects and effects produce circumstances. The circumstances of effects are beyond our control and perpetuate the law of cause and effect. Acceptance of this constant universal motion, should help us to choose kindness as a guide for thought.

Marty: I think that I follow your logic. Anyway, it had not occurred to me that we should apply the principle of sowing and reaping or the law of cause and effect to the process of every day speaking and thinking.

John-jon: If we speak ill of others (which is a form of attack), give way to greed and envy then such thinking mostly results in a fearful mind. (He pulls out a small notepad.) One teacher put it this way; *"As ye sow, so shall ye reap"* means *"that what you* *believe to be worth cultivating you will cultivate in yourself. Your judgment of what is worthy makes it worthy for you."* It speaks to each person's power of choice. With the activities of each day, we're presented with the options of selecting the courage to side with peace or to follow the darkness of attack (verbal or physical). The intent of our thoughts, reflect our choice of cultivation or growth.

Marty: That's an interesting phrase, *"the courage to side with peace"*. It appears to be the same as the courage to practice forgiveness or like you said the courage to choose kindness as a guide. Seems like the cause and effects of siding with peace could produce a very different world.

THE PRACTICE OF GENERALIZATION

John-jon: You have an inviting welcome banner. Hosting and participating in "Circle of Kindness" gatherings is a wonderful idea.

Marty: Sure, we learn from each other and have a good time with the discussions. But, why stop the train of thought concerning the "law of laws"?

John-jon: Well, it's a really heavy or rich subject. One of those topics that require a bit of focus, mindful thought and daily practice. I've noticed that if we talk too much in this area, many people lose interest and may revert to the familiar, go-to practice of generalization.

Marty: The practice of generalization?

John-jon: Yea, when we become somewhat familiar with a thing just enough to begin making broad, over-generalized assumptions and beliefs about it. It's a stereotyping practice that we use for words, ideas, concepts or for groups of people. In the case of cause and effect, some listen to gain an initial introduction to the concept then decide to generalize without depth of understanding.

Marty: Well, we all generalize, don't we? Isn't it a coping and sometimes survival mechanism that the brain uses to fill-in the gaps of unknown or partial information? Or, am I getting my terms mixed up?

John-jon: You are correct. Generalization or rationalization is important, especially for the young, and undeveloped mind. However, as we decide to mature, greater understanding and growth is gained from causation level discussions. A decision to open ourselves to understanding and practicing cause and effect assessment is to **allow ourselves to grow beyond the defensive and reactive forms of thinking**.

Marty: We do agree that learning to cope, adapt and to survive are important lessons, right?

John-jon: Certainly. Survival is an instinctively necessary priority. **And when we accept the courage to live beyond basic survival, we begin to prosper, to flourish and to blossom as human beings.**

Marty: That's pretty good my friend. In order to thrive, we should grow beyond the immature, defensive, survival based reactive thinking. In fact, you've just touched upon a main purpose for our "Circle of Kindness" discussions. Which is **to openly and kindness discuss worthy topics that help to shape and improve our daily life.**

John-jon: That's wonderful. Conversations that seek understanding and clarity beyond basic belief with a focus on joyful living help to restore communication's ability to unity us.

Marty: I've accepted the fact that **maturity is a decision which is made by each person.** Most believe that age is the primary factor without consideration of each person's power of decision, will and choice.

John-jon: Indeed. Age and mental development are factors however, when given proper information, guidance and trusted mentors, a decision to blossom as a mature being is more likely. Thus, the importance of wisdom-based discussions.

Marty: Okay, what should you do when the person that you're trying really hard to help seem to ignore your advice by making decisions that you know aren't in their best interest?

John-jon: Such lessons are repeated over and over again throughout life until the advisor (be it parent, mentor or friend) learns that a primary lesson in the exchange is for them.

Marty: Okay, you have my attention. Please expound upon your position.

John-jon: Whenever we find ourselves worried, frustrated or angry, we to need simply remember that our thinking is directed in an unhealthy direction. Regarding the mentee relationship, we have the choice to practice siding with peace or attempt to imprison another's will.

(Smiling and curious, Marty places his hand under his chin and replies.)

Marty: That's an interesting thought my friend. I need to think about it.

John-jon: As maturing beings, we must teach ourselves to kindly and clearly share our position or recommendation then allow the recipient, like you said, to practice the power of decision. In this case, to side with peace means to be happy for the person who is exercising their freedom to explore the possibilities of life. Even if the person's decision appears to not be in their best interest. An attempt to forcefully forbid an adult from lawful activities is an attempt to imprison the will of another.

Marty: Okay, I mostly understand your point. And I'm sure we agree that more guidance is needed when it comes to the very young and "inexperienced"?

(Before John-jon could answer, Mac walks up to them with a pleasant smile.)

Mac: What's happening Marty?

(Mac and Marty exchange friendly greetings with a nodding gesture.)

Marty: All is well Mac. How are you today?

Mac: Everything is copasetic my brother.

Marty: Mac, meet my new friend John-jon. John-jon meet Mac Shawdy.

John-jon: Please to meet you, Sir.

(With a smile Mac replies.)

Mac: Nice to meet you. It's been awhile since I've been a sir. A friend of Marty is a friend of mind. Mac is my name, Mac Shawdy is what they call me. And since we're now friends, don't take this the wrong way but, what's up with the repeating name, John-jon? One John wasn't enough?

(John-jon smiles and replies.)

John-jon: Well, they're spelled differently.

Mac: Ah okay. I couldn't tell by the sound of it. Homonyms run in my family too. (They all laugh.) I'm just kidding with ya brother. It's not my business to question a man's handle. Pleased to meet ya.
(John-jon and Mac exchange a bit of an awkward handshake.)

Mac: Marty, what's the word for today?

Marty: Well Mac, looks like I'm getting the word today from my friend John-jon. This brother is a wealth of knowledge and I'm learning as we speak.

Mac: Cool. Okay brother John-J, you got a word to share with me today.

(Caught slightly off-guard, John-jon replies.)

John-jon: Ah sure. I'm fond of the word integrity.

Mac: Yea, me too. **Integrity** is very important. Simply be truthful with yourself. Do the right thing even when no one is watching. It's a reflection of the person's internal state of well-being. Marty and I have talked about it before. You have another for us?

John-jon: Okay, the word kindness is essential and worthy of attention.

Mac: Right, right. I'm with ya. When it comes to kindness, it's the intent and spirit of expression behind the word that makes it so heavenly. Its display is part of the universal language of love. Kindness should be a main ingredient in the heart of each person's life. So, welcome to our circle. Might you have another one for us?

John-jon: Sure, one last word. Wisdom.

Mac: Yes, yes. Wisdom. Drop some knowledge on us.

John-jon: **Wisdom is a gift** which is freely given and available to all for acceptance. **It guides us in how to think, how to act and how to utilize our knowledge, experience, and insight for the collective good of life itself.** It's the gift that many grandparents offer but too few of us seem to accept, receive and give it.

Mac: My man. Marty you're right. The brother's tight. You brothers are like a prophet and a preacher hanging out together.
(They all share a laugh.)

Mac: Let me get out of the way so you can learn Marty. Plus, you know I'm kinda particular about my seat in the circle. Good meeting you Brother Prophet. And thank you for sharing.

John-jon: Pleased to meet you Sir.

Mac: Just call me Mac or Mac Shawdy. Mac is my name but Mac Shawdy is what they call me. See you brothers later.
(Mac takes his seat in the circle as others begin to arrive.)

Marty: You just met the almost famous Mac Shawdy. I hope he didn't offend you with the nicknames like John-j or Prophet. He's actually a really nice fellow.

John-jon: No problem. Remember the elders would say, **"it's not always what you do but how you do it."** Some nicknames are shared in the spirit of inspiration with the intention of uplifting. Others are submitted as a form of attack and bullying with the intent of projecting toxic vibes towards another. Generally, we can detect the difference regarding the spirit in which a thing is done. And **regardless of what another may call us, it's most important to know the truth of thyself beyond any name or group affiliation.**

Marty: I'm glad you understand and see things that way. Because unless you tell him that it irritates you, every time Mac sees you, he's probably gonna call you Brother Prophet.

John-jon: He refers to you as Preacher.

Marty: Right. I was an associate at a non-profit organization in mid-town when we met. Now we meet in this circular palace. So, he jokingly calls me Preacher or Brother Preacher. I told him that we see qualities in another because it's in us also. Whatever he calls me, the same thing applies to him.

(A few additional participants have seated themselves and Marty invites John-jon to join the Circle of Kindness discussion.)

Marty: We're just a few minutes away from starting our Circle of Kindness discussion. You are more than welcome to join us.

John-Jon: It would be an honor to join and to listen.

Marty: Great, you'll fit right in. The participates are from all walks of life and many choose to listen. Everyone is equal and the facilitators are selected based on consensus and recommendations. Due to the election of diverse, collaborative leadership, we've grown stronger together in a short time.

John-Jon: It is wonderful to hear your description of the circle and the leadership of "we". It brings to mind a story which highlights the importance of choosing inclusive leadership.

Marty: "We" have just a few minutes before the discussion. Please share your insight regarding leadership.

John-Jon: The story suggests that there are only two kinds of leaders. Leaders who like the game of **chess** and leaders who practice the lessons of the **jigsaw puzzle**.

ONLY TWO KINDS OF LEADERS
(as told by Manuel Pasto)

Leaders who like the game of chess see pieces that are mostly in black and white. **Leaders who enjoy jigsaw puzzles see pieces in many colors understanding that a single piece can be multi-hued.**

In chess, some pieces are far more important than others. Compare a queen's power to that of a pawn.
Comparatively, every piece of the jigsaw puzzle is important. It's very frustrating when you get to the end and 1 or 2 pieces are missing.

In chess, you get ahead by knocking someone off their territory.

With the jigsaw puzzle, you get ahead by putting the pieces together so seamlessly that you don't know where one ends and another begins.

In chess, the object is to win while another loses.
With the jigsaw puzzle, the object is to complete the tapestry.

Many of us have been playing way too much **chess** and not enough jigsaw puzzles.

Marty: That's a wonderful story which highlights the proper mindset for leadership. Thank you for sharing it. I will share it with as many who care to listen. It's now time to join the circle.

(John-Jon joins the circle and sees the Young Lady from the train station waving hello.)

Chapter 6: The Circle of Kindness Discussion

Marty welcomes everyone to the community discussion. Due to a few new participants, he shares a little background on the circle discussion.

Marty: Greetings everyone and welcome to the "Community Circle of Kindness." Thank you for joining us and know that each person is appreciated. With respect for the new participants, I'll share a brief introduction regarding the circle gathering.

The circle is an opportunity for us to communicate, collaborate and to commune with one another regarding everyday life impacting items. It's a meeting place for anyone in the community to come and share in the good news. It's a respectful, open discussion that's fluid, changing and alive with participation from all whom chose to engage.

Similar to a cordial family discussion, however different in that we come from various backgrounds and walks of life. **The primary goal is to share insight and knowledge with one another in the direction of kindness and in the artistry of living our best life.**

It's okay if we disagree. A new friend told me that, well intended discussions look to move beyond thoughts of right or wrong. **It's generally more productive to meet the person where they are by acknowledging or recognizing their position then grow the conversation forward.**

The chairs are placed in a circular manner to reflect the fact that we are all equal. Equal teachers, learners, collaborators and leaders. None here are any greater, nor any less than another.

Part of the task as facilitator is to ensure that the conversations flow, therefore allowing us to maximize our time together.

We're not here to debate, to convince anyone or to sale anything beyond the beauty of kindness in action. Another objective is to share in a manner that is uplifting and encourages all to live in a more positive direction.

Here we remind each other that it's healthy to unplug or to disconnect from the phones and online activities for a while. All are encouraged to simply turn off the technology and engage with the folks who are here and present.

Are there any questions regarding the basics of the circle?

New participant: I have a question or a concern. You talked about turning off our phone. I can't do that. It's important that my family and work associates be able to reach me.

Marty: Thank you for sharing your concern and I understand your position. I too was under this mindset at one time. To disconnect is a recommendation that's suggested with the health and well-being of each person in mind. We are all leaders. As leaders, a beneficial approach may be to view our family and team members as capable leaders. Leaders who are getting better each day.

Remember that tomorrow nor the next hour is promised to anyone. So, the team is better when solid contingency plans have been established in the event of our unavailability. We'll soon have a discussion that's mostly focused on **the practical aspects of leadership.** If you chose not to turn your device off, we kindly ask that you place them in silent mode. Is this a sufficient response to your concern?

New participant: I understand your recommendation.

Marty: Okay, one last thing, we are all here to share and to learn. These kind gatherings have taught us that no one person has all the answers. However, collectively we can positively move awareness of concepts and concerns forward.

Again, it's okay if we disagree. I think it was Aristotle or Plato or one of the ancient thinkers who said, *"It's the mark of an educated and maturing mind to be able to entertain a thought without accepting it."*

OPEN FOR DISCUSSION

Marty: With that said, I now open the floor for discussion.

(The participants were quiet, so Marty offered a topic for exchange.)

Marty: Okay, it appears that we're in listen mode for now. So, I suggest an initial discussion topic that can offer guidance yet is often the source of misunderstandings. They can help bring peace or to provoke anger. (He smiles and says.) Okay, hold on a minute as we pause for dramatic effect.

"**Words**". The suggested topic is words. We often hold loosely, generalized meanings for words which are okay for some situations but not for all. At the surface level, words help to facilitate communication. Along with body language and gestures, we use them in an effort to express our thoughts, feelings and emotions.

And when we are really paying attention, we're trying to understand the meaning, or the feelings being expressed behind the words. Please allow me to share the following quote from an insightful teacher and then we'll listen for your comments.

The Wisdom of Kindness

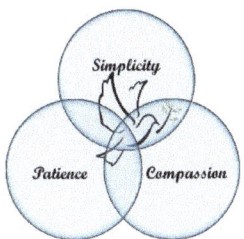

"If we understood the power of our thoughts, we would manage them more closely. If we understood the awesome power of our words, we would prefer silence to almost anything negative. In our thoughts and words, we create our own weaknesses and our own strengths. Our limitations and joys begin in the heart of our mind. We can always replace negative with positive."
(interpretation of Betty Eadie' quote)

Marty: With that said, are there any words that standout for you today that you wished your younger self had understood, accepted and leveraged its meaning sooner?

Mac: Sure, Marty. The word for me is **laughter**. Learning how to laugh with people and never at someone was a big lesson for me. Playing the dozens as a youngster taught several of us some painful lessons. So, I really enjoy comedians with the courage and skill to poke fun at themselves. Remember Rodney Dangerfield's one liners?

Marty: Certainly, some of us do Mac. And I know you do a nice Rodney impersonation. Will you share a few of his one-liners with us?

Mac: I don't mind at all. (Mac stands up and gestures as if adjusting an imaginary necktie just as Rodney was known to do.)

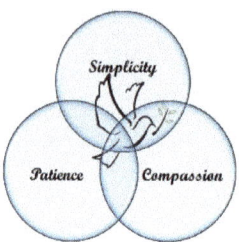

"I had it tough as a kid. I tell ya, I got no respect".
"When I was born, I was so ugly the doctor slapped my mother."
"I could tell my parents hated me. My bath toys were a toaster and a radio."
"My psychiatrist told me I was crazy and I said I want a second opinion. He said okay, you're ugly too."
"I told my dentist my teeth are going yellow. He told me to wear a brown tie."
"I tell ya, I get no respect."

Marty: Okay, thank you kindly Mac. *"As soap is to the body, so laughter is to the soul."*

Mac: I tell ya *"I get no respect".*
"When I was a kid, I got no respect. I had no friends. I remember the see-saw. I had to keep runnin' from one end to the other."
"When I played hide-and-seek. They wouldn't even look for me."
"I tell ya when I was a kid, all I knew was rejection. My yo-yo, it never came back!"
"Me and my dad used to play tag, he'd drive!"
"When I was a kid, I got no respect. When I went on the roller coaster, my old man told me to stand up straight."
"When I was a kid my parents moved a lot, but I always found them."
"It was the same thing in the army, no respect. They gave me a uniform that glowed in the dark."

Marty: Okay, thank you kindly once again Mac. In his own humorous way, Rodney was **telling us to not take anything personally and that we can rise above any situation.** Who knows, it may be true that he overcame a difficult childhood to become a very humorous contributor to life.

Is there anyone else that would like to share a **word which stands out for you today that you wished your younger self had understood its meaning?**

Woman-in-tie-dye-shirt: The days of youth. (while glancing towards the sky) It really does seem that we don't realize what we have until it's gone. Doesn't it? The word that comes to mind for me is **responsibility**. I wish I'd connected with the fact of life that's represented by the word responsibility in my youth.

Mac: By responsibility are you referring to the requirements of a job, or a legal obligation? Or the lack of responsibility when a person is unwilling to commit to basic life-enhancing foundational items for fear of missing out on something? Because, I can relate to this one.

Woman-in-tie-dye-shirt: I completely agree that every adult must accept responsibility for providing and caring for them self. But more specifically, I'm referring to the fact of recognizing **our responsibility to educate ourselves** and to accept **the freedom that maturity offers.** When we accept the responsibility of maturity and freedom, we release many of the unsupported fear-based beliefs.

Marty: You share a really good point. It's each person's responsibility to educate them self as maturity is a choice and a decision.

THE CONCEPT OF ENOUGH

Man-in-dress-shirt: The word or concept that I was slow to grasp its meaning was **"enough"**. I was very slow to understand it, so the lessons were painful. I don't recall seeing movies or hearing many discussions on the subject.

Man-wearing-a-kufi: Yes, yes, understanding **the abundance of enough** has proven difficult for many of us. Without proper guidance, individuals, corporations and even nations fail to recognize and live from the wisdom of enough. The movies and conversations mostly hint about the dangers of greed which is the opposite of enough.

Man-in-dress-shirt: Right. I was so focused on getting more and more stuff that I was overlooking the most important aspects of life. Without understanding the meaning of enough, I fell headfirst into the pitfalls of greed, envy, jealousy, impatience and **the strut of arrogance**. You name the vice and I unfortunately lived it.

Mac: (With an audible laugh.) Ha-ha, that's a good one. I've not heard the strut of arrogance before. I'll remember to use it sometime.

Marty: What caused you to wake up?

Man-in-dress-shirt: I slowly started to recognize the useless impulsive behaviors of always wanting more stuff and things. It started as a nice hobby to find good deals. Later, it grew into an almost uncontrolled desire for almost anything that the commercials or other folks said was valuable. Then the storage problems of where to keep all the stuff and the mental stress of protecting it along with other health problems started to show up.

Mac: Ah, you finally recognized the over-sold, commercialized, wrongheaded, keep up with the Joneses propaganda that's associated with **the manufactured happy**. Back in the day we used to call this a trick bag.

Young-man-in-hoodie: (smiling) What's manufactured happy?

Mac: It's the commercials that tell you over and over again that happiness is found in some product. The messages are repeated so much that we actually start to believe that happiness can be found in a drink, a pill, a house, a car, a food product, or some vacation spot. Drink this, smoke that, go there and you'll find happiness. Hype, all exaggerated hype.

Young-man-in-hoodie: Okay, what's a trick bag?

Carla: It's a hoax, a scheme, a deceptive manipulation. You know, a trick. When something is misleadingly represented as good, healthy and normal. I finally started to notice the trickster-like, deceptive advertisements also. They usually start with some familiar music and a festive party-like scene. Then they hit you with the seemingly innocent product or service that fits right in with the artificially, hyped-up lifestyle. If you pay attention to the advertisements that target kids, the illusionary happy fantasy stuff becomes very clear. Yes, it's just hype.

Man-in-dress-shirt: Well, I fell for it and spent many years chasing an illusion that was unhealthy and not in my best interest. The thoughtless party life of all night is alright, bigger this, more of that and a can't-get-enough mindset, lead me to the empty place of poor health, depression and loneliness.

Marty: Isn't it interesting that the commercialized good times are associated with eating and drinking things that are known to cause sickness and poor health?

Mac: Sure, too much rotgut and muck in your life can't help but lead to the blues. I'm speaking from experience. Sometimes, it takes a while for us to learn what's good for us. I'm what you call a late bloomer.

Man-in-dress-shirt: I learned the hard way also. I guess **the affliction of greed and self-destruction is the result of not learning the lessons of enough. Now, the goal is to build a legacy of truthfulness, courage and kindness.** That's what I'm all about.

Marty: It's said that we pay for our lessons. **Looks like the cost of living with kindness and truth might be to release the illusions of getting and chasing.** Unfortunately, for some, the definition of success is still "he or she who dies with the most stuff wins." With experience, we've learned that more things and stuff, generally means more worries and troubles.

LIVING OUR BEST LIFE

Carla: Marty, I like the subject but, could we go in a slightly different direction for a moment?

Marty: Sure Carla. What's up?

Carla: Well, I had a really interesting discussion at the train station this morning with the gentleman sitting directly across from me. He shared some suggestions in reference to **living our best life** and I'd like to ask a couple of follow-up questions. I think it's a worthy discussion for all to hear.

Marty: Oh, you've met Brother John-jon already. Well, if he's good with your request, we're good.
(All looked to John-jon for a response.)

John-jon: It was a joy to speak with you earlier. Please share your questions.

Carla: You suggested that we practice excellence in several fundamental areas of daily living. Life activities such as eating, exercising, thinking and a couple of others. I understand the need for improved eating and exercising, please remind me of the other items.

John-jon: You are correct, the choice to consciously grow our appreciation for healthy life practices in the areas of **eating, sleeping, exercising, and thinking** are essential to living our best life. To fully mature or "blossom" as a human being, these are among the things that we should cultivate and establish intimate relationship.

Carla: Might you have any practical suggestions to help improve our lifestyles or activities in these areas?

Man-wearing-a-kufi: I recall an ancient Egyptian Proverb that states, *"One quarter of what you eat keeps you alive, the other three quarters, keeps your doctor alive."* This probably led the ancient Greeks to say; *"let food be thy medicine."*

Mac: I really like that one. For many of us, this part of life is fairly simple.
If you don't want to run, don't run. Soon it'll be difficult to run.
If you don't want to walk, then don't walk. Soon it will be difficult to walk.
If you don't want to be healthy, then eat and drink a bunch of sugary, salty junk. Soon your health will start to fail.
My grandma used to say, "Son, do you know what's good for ya? If, so, then keep it simple and do just that."

Marty: Adding to your thought Mac, if we don't want to think in the direction of kindness, then simply continue to distract ourselves with mindless entertainment and allow fearfulness to have its way. Soon it will become difficult to engage in meaningful positive dialogue and action. Without commitment and practice, the ability to live a wonderful life will escape us.

PRACTICE DIRECTIONAL THINKING

John-jon: Precisely. When we **practice living consciously and kindly**, we learn to **respond to situations instead of reacting.** When we practice eating consciously, we **select healthy food as it is viewed as fuel for the body instead of enslavement to the conditioned taste buds.**

Mac: Eating should be pretty straight forward and obvious. Garbage-in, garbage-out. We simply need to take the few seconds needed to review the ingredients of what's being put in our one and only body. It's interesting that we have some really intelligent people that do really "unwise" stuff when it comes to nutritious eating and managing the fundamentals of health.

Woman-in-tie-dye-shirt: Sometimes it takes a while before we realize the level of propaganda and conditioning that has helped to shape our basic life habits. You also mentioned another difficult life impacting item that we all face. Learning how to respond, instead of reacting to situations.

John-jon: Yes, it makes sense to practice the things that we want to improve. **In a sense, all of life may be considered a practice in directional thinking.** What seems like many options and choices are but two. Either our thinking, acting, talking and **behavior is oriented in the direction of the light or away from the light.**

Woman-in-tie-dye-shirt: I mostly understand your point, but please share what you mean by "the light."

John-jon: We use many different words such as love, compassion, peace, joy, pleasantness and kindness to represent the light. Conversely, words such as evil, hatred, prejudice, attack, greed and fear are used to represent thoughts and actions which are away from the light or towards darkness.

Man-in-dress-shirt: Humm, that's interesting. Earlier, you used the phrase "intimate relationship". I'm not sure that I've seen the phrase intimate relationship paired with basic life activities. Mostly, you only hear the phrase associated with the interaction between two people. And your concept of directional thinking seems a bit too simple. Please share a bit more context regarding your "thoughts".

John-jon: It makes sense to embrace, understand and **establish healthy best practices around the basic fundamentals of life.** It's a concept practiced by the infant who forms an intimate relationship with its breastfeeding mother. **That which sustains and allows us to function in a whole and healthy manner is worthy of**

attention and focus. If we can accept that *"life is a journey, not a destination"*, then **the direction of our thoughts greatly influences the quality of the perceived journey.** Thus, an important intimate relationship is to embrace the practice of directional thinking along with the acceptance and appreciation of life itself.

Man-in-dress-shirt: Your point is well received. I've also quoted Emerson on many occasions. If for example, life was a destination then we'd probably go in the opposite direction to avoid reaching the end. So yes, I agree that life is a journey, therefore the direction that we allow ourselves to think does matter. Thank you for the insight.

Woman-in-tie-dye-shirt: I'm enjoying the conversation. It's not new information but it is a reminder that there's a better way of thinking and living if we choose to accept it. It's also really nice to hear people talking about positive things in this manner without any required attachments.

Mac: Right on. Here in the circle, we have practical conversations to live by. We're free to try the suggestions to see if they'll help or simply let them go down the river Lethe with all the other forgotten thoughts.

John-jon: You make a good point. It is possible that we can't forget some things as the lessons within them may be very helpful to life's journey if viewed or received properly. The past may simply be for us to learn and to become better, not bitter.

Marty: I really like your recommendation to practice "directional thinking". When we find ourselves upset or angry at something or someone, remembering to practice this concept can help to quickly re-orient our thinking in a healthier direction.

Lady-in-purple-dress: I agree that it is refreshing to speak with others in the affirmative. But how does this help with all of the violence, the crime and the addiction problems?

Mac: That's a good question Brother Prophet. How can such big brain creatures keep falling for the same old tricks? Like she said, the violence, the crime, addictions and the generational misguided thinking that's associated with the excessive greed, the unfairness around gender, and skin tonality. I don't call it skin color because no two people have the exact same skin tone. Is it possible that in spite of a big brain, in a sense, might we be one of the dumbest creatures to walk the planet?

John-jon: A big brain does not mean that one cannot be trained and conditioned for unhealthy thinking, therefore behavior. The elephant's brain is about 4 times the size of humans, still it can be trained. **When we are ready for a solution, then we begin to open the mind and train ourselves to focus on the cause instead of chasing the effects of a situation.**

Man-in-dress-shirt: So, are we too smart for our own good? Are we allowing our intellect to become a liability?

Man-wearing-a-kufi: What all the negativity shows is that we're capable learners. It's a matter of **right learning, wrong teaching.** I say that **the generational behavior of bullying, arrogance, greed and corruption which promotes poverty and moral failure are examples of right learning but wrong teaching.** As kids and throughout life, we correctly learn the things that are seen and "practiced" before us.

John-Jon: Rightly said my friend. Unfortunately for the people, the economic system that has been repeatedly thrusted upon society is structured to pit small identity segmented groups against each other. The uncaring distractions of inequality and our misguided emotional energies are used to direct attention away from how illogical and insane the financial system is structured. Plainly stated, an economic system that is based upon the fabrication of scarcity is inherently unjust and unfair. It appears to have been organized and constructed over time to elevate a few at the expense of many.

Marty: Very interesting. So, it's not necessarily the love of money as the root of all evil. It's the idea and belief that some are more worthy of care than another because of a faulty accounting system. It's greed, fear and the evil or corruption of classism that we should be mindful to withdraw support.

Man-wearing-a-kufi: You're saying what most people already know in their heart. Allowing those who by various means have acquired a mass of financial resources to buy the allegiance and influence of policymakers is a foolhardy system. Many aspects of our slowly evolving political and financial systems are counter-productive, destructive and unwise.

Mac: I agree that as the economic system is currently constructed, it's not in the best interest of the majority of the people. But how has it been maintained for so long?

John-Jon: A system will change when enough people are committed to changing it. There's a short familiar story that gives insight to the power of training and conditioning which helps to promote generational behavior.

A young girl recalls watching the elephant trainers work with the animals and noticed that some were tied up with only a small rope around their front leg. When the opportunity presented itself, she asked the trainer, how can that small rope hold such a big elephant? The trainer replied, when they are very young, we use the same size rope to restrain them and at that age the rope is strong enough to hold them. Over time the animal becomes conditioned to believe that it can't break free. Even after it has physically grown three or four times its initial size, it holds to the belief that it can't break free of the "once stronger" rope.

The young girl asked; but why don't they just try to break free again? The trainer replied, belief left unchallenged and unvalidated on a regular bases can limit the freedoms of an elephant's mind or a human being. It's also important to understand that the captor must work to keep the powerful creatures reasonably comfortable or it will become surly or ill-tempered and subsequently break free of the mental binder. Do you understand?

The young girl replied; I think so. As he was walking away, the trainer turned and said; Oh, there's one more important component to keeping the powerful creatures contented. It's also very helpful if the young one's see that the older animals have also accepted the same binding condition. The animals are trained until they become self-regulating in the subservient manner which they have been trained. So, make a note to yourself, learn to identify and to consistently validate the beliefs and customs that seem to guide your daily thinking as they serve to shape the perception of your reality.

Remember, you have the ability to free yourself from any situation. Simply embrace learning and train yourself to practice life with the courage to examine your habits and beliefs. Freedom can be gained from mostly any situation, even the mental binders of conditioned servitude.

Mac: I like that Brother Prophet. "We have the ability to free ourselves from any situation. Simply have the courage to examine our beliefs, grow in knowledge and kept trying each day."

Young-man-in-hoodie: He said, "embrace learning and train our self to practice life with the courage to examine our habits and beliefs."

Mac: Dig that! You're right, young blood. The brother has made his point a couple of times that the important things in life should be practiced if we want to improve them. Everything is copasetic.

THE SMALL IDENTIDIES OF I

Carla: I have one last question. This morning, you also mentioned the small identities of I. What did you mean by this?

John-jon: What we believe about ourselves matters greatly. Earlier, the misguided and erroneous thoughts associated with the hue of one's skin was rightly noted.

It is very possible that the over-identification with small identities such as gender, ethnicity, group affiliation, occupation, nationality and perceived social status may be primary contributors to the continuation of our harmful economic system. The effects of such a system is the perception and acceptance of global despair, misery and constant war.

Carla: All those things that you're calling small identities, are primary features and attributes which are used as identification.

Woman-in-tie-dye-shirt: Actually, as I reflect on the list of items, it appears that those are categories or groupings that are used to classify, stereotype and to separate people. None of them actually speak to the character or essence of the person.

John-jon: To paraphrase a wonderful teacher, **"How do you think of yourself within your heart?"** Are we the **"wholly lovable and loving"** being from our Creator? Or are we the accumulation of thoughts, images, small group affiliations, and experiences that we each cling to and declare our allegiance?

Man-in-dress-shirt: I understand that you're suggesting that we don't allow the surface-level, outward characteristics to define how we think about ourselves. But many people devote a lot of time and energy into strengthening their identification with these very things.

"KNOW THYSELF"

John-jon: We could speak at length regarding **the adoption of small identities and the masks that we use to cover or hide our truth**. It's very likely that **our most important journey as a physical embodiment of life-energy is towards understanding the truth of "thyself"**. The direction for attaining such truth is always inward towards the eternal light of life.

Marty: Several of us have discussed Socrates famous proclamation for us to, **"Above all else know thyself"** and *"the unexamined life is not worth living."* It's an ongoing, open-ended discussion.

John-jon: Leveraged properly, the masks of small identities can represent a victory for the strength in diversity, the positivity of inclusiveness and our ability to overcome any form of discrimination.

Young-man-in-hoodie: Hold on a minute. I agree with her, the things that you listed as small identities (gender, race, religion, group affiliation, country) make up a person's identity. If you're saying something different, then I don't understand.

John-jon: Those things are okay as long as we remember to keep the main thing as the main thing. In this case, **the main thing which is to be respected, appreciated and celebrated is life itself. The light of life and the energy of love are the ties which bind everyone and all experiences together. Therefore, love and life are our truth.**

(John-jon appears to pause in thought.)

Mac: Okay, when you pause like that, we know there's more to it. You have our attention.

John-jon: As it relates to life, just because we speak of a thing and become familiar with a name or term that's used to represent it, does not mean that we have understanding of it or that we are fully utilizing its powerful truth. Socrates is also credited with saying, *"True wisdom comes to each us when we realize how little we understand about life, ourselves, and the world around us."*

Young-man-in-hoodie: Okay, I understand. Like you said, when it comes to identification, life is the main thing that we should identify with above any of the smaller attributes and affiliations.

John-jon: Exactly. Another teacher put it this way, *"Not-knowing is true knowledge. Presuming to know is a disease."* Think about how often we thought or presumed to know something just because we read about it or heard others repeat the message a few times. Before we can accept help with this illness, we must realize our lack of awareness and then move toward truth. A short, slightly humorous but reasonable story comes to mind.

(There was a pause of silence.)

Carla: Okay, we understand. Are you going to share the story? Is it the one about "The Blind Men and the Elephant" that you mentioned this morning?

John-jon: Please pardon me. The ancient allegory that you mentioned is an excellent one. If accepted and received properly, it can provide insight into the value of diversity and respect for each person's point of view. It also implies that with collaboration and our collective perspective, we can gain a larger vision, appreciation and greater understand regarding the enormity of truth, love and of life.

Young-man-in-hoodie: That sounds interesting. Can you share the "slightly humorous" story then flow with the blind men that show us how to gain a larger vision of life?

John-jon: Certainly. The story is titled, **"What does life look like?"**

WHAT DOES LIFE LOOK LIKE?

After the funeral of a young friend, a curious child asked some of the attendees the following question, "What does life look like?"

Excuse me Sir, I saw my friend in the casket today. Does life and death look the same? Because my friend still looks the same as he did before the death got him. Does death and life look the same?

Oh no, most certainly not. The only reason the person in the casket looks the same is because the morticians did a good job of preparing the body. When a person dies, they become cold, rigid, and stiff. To this the child said; but grandma asks grandpa why he's so cold, rigid and stiff in his thinking. Sir, does my grandpa have the death? Of course not, your grandpa is very much alive. He's standing right over there.

The child then approached two people whom were talking. Excuse me, my friend died and that man told me what the death is like. Can you tell me what life looks like? Why certainly. Just look around, you see all these people, that dog assisting its owner, and those plants over there? That's what life looks like.

The other person chimed in and said, just a moment. You pointed out objects and things that have life within them. People, animals, and plants are alive because the energy of life is within them. As I understand it, life is the spirit which enliven the person, the animal and the plants. With this understanding, I'm not sure there's a clear answer to the child's question. Do you understand what I'm saying young one?

I'm not sure. Looks like people can agree on the feel of death but it's kinda hard for them to agree on the face of life.

(The wind picks up again and it begins to drizzle.)

Marty: That's a very interesting story my friend. It's one that we should probably give a bit more thought. Thank you and thank you too all the participants for sharing and engaging in an informative and insightful discussion. With respect for time and for the weather, we will conclude today's dialogue. I've taken a few notes and will share a recap at our next discussion.
We started today with an open discussion on words and I'd like to close with this short poem by an unknown author.

"Words are seeds that do more than blow around. They land in our hearts and not the ground. Be careful what you plant and careful what you say. You might have to eat what you planted one day."
(Unknown)

Marty: Finally, the big community celebration is in a few weeks. So, Ruben and friends will be hosting our next discussion at the mid-town community center. Thank you all once again and this concludes today's discussion.

Grandma closes the book and shares with the kids that the author is open to suggestions as the book is not yet complete.

Chapter 7: A Family Tradition of Kindness & Joyful Living

Grandma, Grandpa and their three grandkids just finished reading the first part of an unfinished book. The author of the document asked if they would share feedback and suggestions.

Grandma: Well that's the end of the document for now kids. What do you think so far?

Oldest Grandchild: It's different.

Youngest Grandchild: Why are we reading this book? It's just folks talking, and I don't understand everything that they're saying. I like books and movies that have action and adventure.

Oldest Grandchild: Some of the material is a little advanced. I understand most of it but I'm the oldest.

Grandma: We decided to share it with you because the document is designed to encourage more conversations and discussions around some meaningful ideas and concepts. It's okay if you don't understand every aspect of it just yet. This is the type of material that we all must grow into as more insight is gain with each reading and each conversation.

Middle Grandchild: The book was okay. I enjoyed some of the short stories. The part about doing your best was cool.

Grandpa: You're right, kids. Several of the concepts are a bit advanced. Just remain open to the lessons and more clarity will come as you increase in life experiences. So, with your participation, we'd like these types of conversations to become part of our family tradition. **We're suggesting regular discussions on how to think and how to live our best life.**

Grandma: Grandpa and I feel that **the time is right to start a family tradition of having discussions with the focus of helping each person become the best that they can be.** That means discussions on quality words, thinking and how to live joyfully within the moment.

Middle Grandchild: I'm all for it. I want to tell my friends about it. Now, tell me again; what's the main goal for our new family tradition?

Grandpa: We want to **encourage each of you to gracefully mature while growing the content of your character.**

Youngest Grandchild: What does the content of your character mean?

Grandma: The phrase speaks to the mental and moral qualities of an individual. Or, how a person has trained them self to think, act and to behave.

Youngest Grandchild: But I still don't understand.

Grandma: Don't worry honey. In no time at all, you'll be telling us all about the benefits of directional thinking, the problem of over-identification with small identities, and the strength gained from integrity of character.

Middle Grandchild: I'm ready Grandma. When do we get started?

Grandma: On your next visit, we'll discuss how most if not all of the concepts in this small book apply to each of us. Age is really not a factor when it comes to wisdom-based thoughts, teachings and living.

Grandpa: Remember the part about *"know thyself"* and *"life is a journey, not a destination"*? Well, we want to help you, ***"place yourself in charge of the journey, where you and only you must remain."***

Grandma: We want to help you become the best version of yourself. Recall the book's subtitle **"The Direction for Living Our Best Life".** The document speaks of more than just the words, but the feelings and emotions that we are trying to express with the words.

Grandpa: The author is open for suggestions. What is it that you'd like to see in the next document?

Youngest Grandchild: More action and adventure.

Middle Grandchild: Relationships. I'd like to learn about relationships.

Oldest Grandchild: Money. How to become rich.

Grandpa: Please understand that we're not forcing anything on you. **We view these conversations as an investment in our family's level of joy.** So, will you give it an honest try with us?

Oldest Grandchild: Sure grandpa. It will be a pleasure to learn with you and grandma.

Middle Grandchild: I'm ready.

Youngest Grandchild: I guess so.

Grandma: Wonderful. Thank you, kids. We'll discuss the topics noted in the book again. Just remember that all of life is a practice and there are only two directions for thinking and living. Either our thoughts, words, and actions are directed towards the light of kindness or away from its light. This new tradition is our gift to each of you. So, understand that **we wish you more than happiness, we wish you the consistency of joy.**

Grandpa: Kids, consider these conversations as part of your wisdom-based education. Here's a quote for you; *"Those who lack wisdom are children. Children do confuse fantasy and reality, and they are frightened, because they do not know the difference."*

Oldest Grandchild: Grandpa, why do people use quotes all the time?

Grandpa: Probably for different reasons. When I use them, it's because *"I like what the person said and how they said it."* (smiling with a small laugh.) That too is a quote.

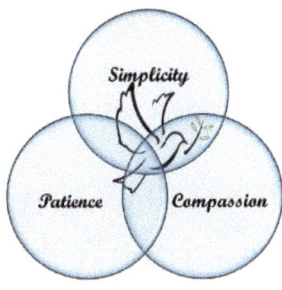

Many will read, some will discuss but few will receive wisdom's teachings as a call to personal action.

Our growth and maturity unfold and strengthens with each act of kindness. Be encouraged to sow the seeds of kindness with positive words, actions and deeds. Such small actions bear fruit far beyond our awareness.

Chapter 8: Conclusion (for now)

A Joyful Journey

The river as it streams towards the ocean,

The migrating herd following the rains to fresh grasslands,

And the mind that allow its thoughts to flow in the direction of love's eternal light,

All demonstrate the wisdom of kindness and consistently experience the joy of living a wonderful life.

The light of life and the energy of love are the ties which bind everyone and all experiences together. Therefore, love and life are our truth.

The Wisdom of Kindness

The wisdom of kindness is a gift which is freely given and available to all for acceptance. It guides us in how to think, how to act and how to utilize our knowledge, experience, and insight for the collective good of all life.

"A journey without miles to a destination that doesn't change." And, *"all things take shape, become active, then return to their source."* Both truisms relate to and are associated with the experience of life. With this understanding, a worthy goal might be to live a quality, meaningful life that's filled with an abundance of happiness, health, kindness, care, and joy. Not only is such a wonderful life possible, we were created for the adventure and are perfectly equipped to thrive within it.

Virtuous stories, teachings, and parables offer us examples of how to think, therefore, how to live. To allow ourselves to experience the fulness of life, we need only open our awareness to the direction of wisdom's guidance and journey with the vision of kindness.

Likely, everything which comes to our awareness is for us to become better. We analyze, intellectualize, interpret, discuss and even give recommendations but fail to accept the moral lessons within the situation for our own self-improvement. In a sense, it's like preparing a wonderful meal over and over again but deciding not to receive its nourishing blessings. We've conditioned ourselves to talk about situations, circumstances and one another without accepting that the lessons being displayed are for us. **Remember the young lady at the train station who witnessed another passenger offer his seat in attempt to defuse a quarrel?** Generally, we choose to focus attention on the sparkle or disruption of dramatic circumstance while overlooking the wisdom for model behavior. Situations, like people come to teach us things to do and things not to do. With the wisdom of kindness, we gain the proper mindset for living our best life.

It is our life's purpose to mature into a joyful, kind and loving being. Simply resolve to "do our best" in gaining awareness and acceptance of wisdom's truth.

Perhaps the major difference in our life's journey is the perception in which we allow ourselves to view past experiences and our belief or un-belief in what is possible. Wisdom shares that our accepted beliefs and perceptions are shaped by us and our internal chosen companion for processing thought. *"As a man thinketh in his hearth, so shall he be."*

It has been expressed that there are but two primary emotions which serve as counsel for thought; love and fear. *"Each is a way of seeing, and different worlds arise from their different visions."* Equally, there are two perspectives for living; inward, toward our eternal light and outward toward a shifting, changing world. **Recall the story of the man and his lost keys?** The man knew that his keys were inside but decided to search outside under the lights anyway. Similarly, we understand that love, joy and compassion are within us, but oftentimes choose to search outward, toward worldly things anyway.

We understand that the past has passed and we're only bound by it if we chose to be. The decision to live in the present is liberating and is the only place where freedom is found and experienced. With the strength of humility and the resolve of forgiveness, we can release yesterday's grievances and begin living more abundantly in the powerful present.

> *"Free of the past, we begin to see that love is within us, and we have no need to look without where we thought it was."*

Know that it is we who bring the joy, the peace, the kindness and the compassion to the experiences of life as they are all sourced from the well of abundance within the self.

A decision to journey inward towards love's light is to practice living everyday activities with the wisdom of kindness leading the way towards our return to innocents. The result of such thinking is release of the mind from the chains of fear, guilt and shame. Remember, **all action is preceded by thought.** Therefore, it is our chosen thought-system that helps to shape and co-create the perception of our life's experiences. With our acceptance of love's counsel, joy becomes the new foundation for doing, living and being.

So, relax and enjoy the fact that without our help, the sun continues to shine, water still renews, and the next breath will help to sustain. Understand that we are much more than the imperfections of the memory and the crafted personalities which are associated with our many small identities. With the simple power of decision, we can experience life beyond the negative thoughts of self-doubt and the institutionalized categories of ethnicity, skin tonality, sexism, tribalism, nationalism, and classism. *"In truth, we share our life because we have one Source."*

"Possibly, the greatest adventure within each life's journey is the maturing, the opening up, the growing and the blossoming process itself." The physical transformation of the child to adulthood may be a small reflection of our capacity for mental and moral growth into a pleasant representation of life. Each of us decide when it's time to mature, to train the mind and to step into the greatness of our being. Until that moment, to the kind observer, we appear like the little boy with the clay who said, *"I just wanna PLAY WITH it for a minute!!!"*

"The powerful mind can be perceived like that of a team of horses. Let the reins go, and the horses will drag you down. Anyone can do that, but the ones who practice learning to direct the powerful horses are the stronger ones. Which requires the greater strength, letting go, or will power?" The ones who let go, train the mind to think in reaction to situations. Those who practice responding to situations (self-control) under the guidance of wisdom, kindness, and patience are most powerful.
(paraphrased eastern teaching)

For consistency of joy, we must train our mind to recognize thoughts, words, and actions which are sourced from the guidance of love and release those without love's light. *"A main purpose for our learning is to enable us to bring the peace with us while helping to heal distress and turmoil."* Train the mind and it will serve us wonderfully. Fail to train it, then thoughts of lack, want, misery and despair enter the uncared-for space.

Remember the little boy practicing his basketball skills? His goal was to become excellent at basketball and life. The suggestion was to always "do the right thing" as it relates to virtuous living and to simply "do your best". *"The goal is to practice being the best that you can be while living a joyful life with integrity and kindness as your guide."* Resolve to establish positive habits for nurturing life's physical and essential infrastructure items such as *drinking clean water, healthy eating, reasonable sleeping, regular exercise, daily meditation, and the practice of directional thinking.* If our decision is to live wonderfully, then helping each other to practice the fundamentals of life with the wisdom of kindness will allow each of us to gain the quiet confidence and strength of humility.

Reasonably, all experiences may be viewed as collaborative adventures between the thinker and his/her chosen internal council. Therefore, the answerability and accountability for the level of joy experienced within life, starts and ends with each of us. Understandably, with respect to free will of decision, if we weren't free to choose fearfulness, we would not be free to choose collaboration and co-creation with love. Restated, if we were not free to choose poorly, we would not be free to choose wisely.

Viewed more simply, what seems like many options, choices and directions for living are but two. Either our thinking, acting, talking and behavior is oriented in the direction of love's light or away from it. Accordingly, the concept of directional thinking suggest that we consistently teach and train ourselves to practice living with the guidance of wisdom and the vision of kindness. As a result, living under the influence of wisdom and kindness produces fruit such as of peace of mind, pleasantness and an abundance of joy. Such fruit come from the core of our being which is truth, love and the light of life.

With our renewed understanding and accepted relationship with life, we welcome the rebirth of joy. Joyful living is an inside-out expression of maturity. *All life experiences are considered an inside job*.

Recall the elephant trainer's advice to the young girl. We have the ability to free ourselves from any situation. Simply embrace learning and train ourselves to practice life with the courage to examine our habits and beliefs. Freedom can be gained from any situation, even the mental binders of conditioned servitude.

The Wisdom of Kindness

"True wisdom comes to each us when we realize how little we understand about life, ourselves, and the world around us."

We conclude with the ancient story of The Blind Men and the Elephant. As stated, if accepted and received properly, it can provide insight into the value of diversity and respect for each person's point of view. It also implies that with collaboration and our collective perspective, we can gain a larger vision, appreciation and greater understand regarding the enormity of truth, of love and of life.

The Blind Men and the Elephant

A group of blind men heard that a strange animal, called an elephant, had been brought to the village, but none of them were aware of its shape and form. Out of curiosity, they said: "We must inspect and know it by touch, of which we are capable". So, they sought it out, and when they found it, they groped about it.

In the case of the first person, whose hand landed on the elephant's trunk, said "this being is like a thick snake".

As for another person, whose hand was upon its leg, said, "the elephant is a pillar like a tree-trunk."

The blind man who placed his hand upon its side said "the elephant is like a wall". The last one felt the elephant's tail and described it as a rope.

Like many timeless parables, there are multiple lessons to be gained from the story. Each man sought to learn, conceptualize and to describe the object based on their limited experience. Some interpretations of the story portray the men as being suspect that the others were either dishonest, foolish, wrong-minded or just insane.

One moral of the parable *"is that we humans have a tendency to claim absolute truth based on our limited, subjective experience as we ignore other people's limited, subjective experiences which may be equally true."*

This story has likely endured for centuries as the object being examined (the elephant) may be perceived as a metaphor for cultural traditions, truth, life or love. Interestingly, the blind men knew that they could not see but like most of us, they didn't know that they struggle due to lack of vision and understanding of the whole. **When we listen to the best of one another and respond with appropriate follow-up actions, the light of humanity and life seem to shine more brightly.**

What's the point of it all? Why wisdom, kindness and so much talk about our life's journey? Because reasonably, we can accept that tomorrow is not promised, the past cannot be changed and the present is a gift for joyous living. *With renewed focus and discussion on joyful living, our efforts help to restore communication's ability to unity us.* Life is always giving, the question is are we open enough to accept, receive and to give back?

The Wisdom of Kindness

"There is but one shift in perception that is necessary, for we made but one mistake. It seems like many, but it is all the same. What is not love is always fear and nothing else."

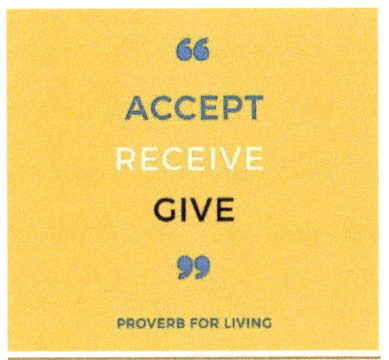

Given the choice of fearfulness or lovingkindness as traveling companions for thought, which do you choose? Understand that a none decision is but self-deception in favor of fearful thinking. Do you choose to give your life to thoughts of misery and despair or to the courage and strength of kindness? Each of us decide and provide evidence with the practiced words, behavior and actions of our daily life.

The Flower of life

"Yesterday I was clever, so I wanted to change the world. Today I am wise, so I am changing myself."

"If you are irritated by every rub, how will you be polished?"

"Your task is not to seek for love, but merely to seek and find all the barriers within yourself that you have built against it."

Rumi
(13th-century mystic poet)

Very little is needed to make a happy life; it is all within yourself, in your way of thinking.
(Marcus Aurelius around 145 AD)

"The stronger cannot help the weaker unless the weaker is willing to be helped, and even then, the weaker must become strong of themselves; they must, by their own efforts, develop the strength which they admire in another. No one but ourselves can alter our condition."
(James Allen)

Each day is a new day, a new beginning. Another opportunity to grow, to mature and to renew the journey of living our best life.

References

The text, quotes and short stories are sourced from the wisdom-well of the ages as shared via the teachings of Buddhism, Christianity, Hinduism, Islam, Judaism, Sikhism, Taoism and all other wisdom-based teachings brought to our awareness. Undoubtedly, the ultimate source for all wisdom is the eternal light of love that dwells within all forms of life.

Additional teachers and documents referenced are:
- **A Course in Miracles (ACIM)**
- **Tao Te Ching, Stephen Mitchell**
- **As a Man Thinketh, James Allen**
- **The Power of Myth, Joseph Campbell**
- **Eastern Philosophy**
- **The mother wit of parents, grandparents, caregiver and friends**
- Ancient African and Egyptian teachings
- Ancient Greek teachings
- Ancient Hebrew teachings
- www.freespeech.org

About the Author

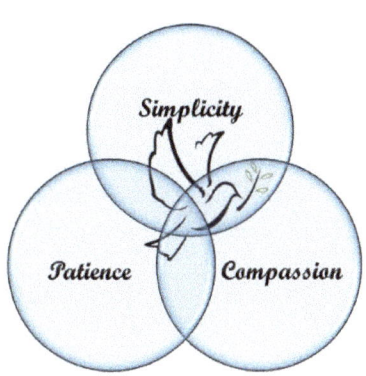

Herb Williams is a native of Memphis, TN with optimism for helping to build winning teams. With this writing, his focus is on helping each individual to positively re-orient their thinking using the simple concept of "directional thinking". His style of delivery is to share truth-based stories and insightful parables from the ages as food for thought in practicing and living our best life. "The Wisdom of Kindness" is designed to help re-introduce wisdom-based discussions of joyful living and kindness of being into our everyday family conversations.

www.ingramcontent.com/pod-product-compliance
Lightning Source LLC
Chambersburg PA
CBHW060931170426
43193CB00027B/2998